CW00719583

HEAL
RELATIONSHIPS

Stop Jealousy and Negative Thinking Through Extraordinary Couple Communication

by SARAH SULLIVAN

Congratulation on purchase this book and thank You for doing so.

Please enjoy *!*

Table of Contents

Introduction

All the things that you expect to grow must be nurtured and taken care of when you expect excellent results. As a couple, your union is no different and, you need to commit yourself to do all you can to ensure that you are ahead in this regard. For your relationship to operate at its optimum, you need to ensure that it is not the collective effort of just one person. You both need to read from the same script and more so be on the same page. When you go through your vows, you say that you become 'one'. This is supposed to be taken literally because your systems should be synchronized. A couple speaking in one voice is a couple that is going places. Since you come from different backgrounds, it might not be always easy to fully understand each other. Nobody is saying that you need to understand each other. You need to start living your lives establishing a new reality together and slowly, you will definitely become one.

In relationships for couples, you must have heard couples saying that they are drifting away from each other yet they sleep in the same bed. Emotional unity and togetherness are going to come about when you follow the above tip. Making the best out of your relationship is not easy yet, with the right mindset, you can do all you want. Let your mindset be anchored on a positivist attitude.

RELATIONSHIP: RECIPE FOR SUCCESS

When considering what goes into a successful marital or other coupling relationship, we might first consider what to leave out of the relationship. Those wanting a successful relationship are well advised to leave such attitudes toward your partner as avoidance, contempt,condescension, scorn, condemnation, ridiculing, disdain, indifference, discourtesy, and manipulation out of the mix.

So, now that we know what ingredients to leave out, let's look at some important ingredients for a successful relationship. Important qualities to possess when one wants a successful relationship are/to be:

Present and Available
Trustworthy
Receptive and Accepting
Respectful
Forgiving
Patient

Understanding
Empathetic
Compassionate

When each person in any relationship makes improvements in these ways of being, the relationship will improve. When positive intentions, good communication skills and a sense of humor are added; the relationship is more likely to flourish. Let's consider each of these ingredients for successful relationships to more fully understand how they impact what is experienced.

Being Present and Available

To be present one has to have their attention in the present time and directed on the other person in the relationship. To be available one has to be ready to participate. When either person in a couple is not mentally in the present and focusing on the other person, it is hard to work on the relationship itself. This is not to say that those in a relationship are in the present and ready to interact with the other partner 24-7.

This is also not to say that a relationship is not enhanced by those times when one partner is in the present and listening to their partner whose attention is focused on the past or the future. In these cases, it is most beneficial when there are agreement and reciprocity. When it is time to focus on the relationship, it is most helpful for both partners to have their attention on the other and be ready to participate.

Being Trustworthy

The level of trust each partner in a relationship has for each other is of paramount importance. When a partner is trustworthy, their partner can rely on their integrity and character as well as be confident that what they say is true. In short, they can be relied upon to speak the truth and do what they say, to the best of their ability. This trust promotes a feeling of safety within the relationship and thus creates fertile ground for relationship success.

Being Receptive and Accepting

Relationship success is further enhanced by each partner's receptivity to and acceptance of the other partner. Positive progress in a relationship is supported when each partner is capable, ready, and willing to receive from the other partner through verbal as well as not verbal means in a good-natured manner with gladness and approval.

Being Respectful
One of the most important qualities for partners to demonstrate to their mates is the giving and receiving of respect. Respect encompasses such qualities as genuine admiration, high opinion, reverence, and value. When we respect someone we hold them in high regard-their comfort and wellbeing are important to us. When the partners start to give particular attention and consideration toward the other, as well as to the relationship itself, by expressing special and high regard; the success of their relationship is enhanced.

Being Forgiving
Besides being genuinely respectful to one another, being forgiving is essential to success in a relationship. In fact, respect and forgiveness are closely tied and work together in tandem. Forgiveness means to excuse ourselves or another for a fault or an offense. Forgiveness can occur only when one chooses to forgive. Our understanding of

forgiveness is enhanced when knowing what it is, what it is not, and how it is facilitated.

Forgiveness is not:

- Believing something that happened is acceptable when it is not
1. Condoning or excusing any unkind, inconsiderate, or selfish behavior

Forgetting something happened
- Denying or minimizing hurt

Forgiveness is:

- Releasing our past to heal our present
- Beneficial and healing to the forgiver because it gives power, energy, peace of mind and
- control of feelings -especially anger and resentment-- back to the forgiver
- Available any time whether solicited or not

Forgiveness is facilitated by:

- Being responsible for one's own thoughts and feelings
- Understanding that we can only really control ourselves
- Keeping our expectations for ourselves and others realistic
- Being relaxed and at the moment, as much as possible
- Being Patient

In the course of living we find that besides being respectful and forgiving, we sometimes need to be patient with our partner. We often hear "Patience is a virtue," So what is patience and how does a relationship become more successful with more of it? One dictionary definition of patience is: having endurance and even calmness under difficult circumstances, which can mean persevering in the face of delay or provocation without acting on annoyance or anger in a negative way. Clearly, I am not talking about being patient with abuse and suggest getting outside assistance if our partner is exhibiting abusive conduct.

What I am talking about is, as, in forgiveness, we have realistic expectations of our partner. Hopefully, we have aired our "non-negotiable" lifestyle issues before getting thoroughly involved. When I think of patience, I am reminded of a quote from an anonymous source; "Between stimulus and response, there is a space. In that space lies our freedom and power to choose our response. In our response lies our growth and our happiness." If we miss something important in the dating/courting process and have been patiently attempting to work it out together, as much as we are capable in a situation; we can ask our partner to go to therapy to resolve the issue and gain more understanding of our partner and our self.

Being Understanding

A partner understands when he/she comprehends and accepts his/her mate's susceptibilities, tendencies, and inclinations. Understanding occurs when each partner is thoroughly familiar with their mate's character and propensities and grasps the meaning and nature of their partner. The safety needed for a truly healthy relationship occurs when each partner understands and empathizes with the others qualities, struggles, and true self and commits to stay in the relationship and work out any issues that may arise between them during their lives together.

Being Empathetic

When a partner empathizes they do not actually have the same feeling as their partner in any given situation. They do however identify with the partner's feelings. Each partner is equipped to empathize with their partner to the degree that they are able to feel and identify with their own feelings. Empathizing includes the ability to psychologically put one's self in the place of another. As when we know our partner hears what we say to them; when our partner is empathetic towards us, we feel heard and understood and thus safer and more comfortable in our relationship.

Being Compassionate

Being compassionate towards our partner goes past empathy and understanding and includes an instinctive selfless insight and feeling of deep sympathy and sorrow for mankind's as well as our partner's misfortunes, trials, and tribulations. Compassion includes hints of a hard to explain capacity within us that makes us more likely to want to assist our partner in coping with tragedy or discomfort. As opposed to rescuing, healthy compassion includes supportive assistance which allows the partner to feel as empowered as possible to do whatever his/her capacity allows rectifying the situation. As with empathy, the capacity to be compassionate is dependent on one's own self-awareness and feeling of connectedness to humankind.

One may ask; "If we put all the ingredients you mentioned into our relationship will it be successful?" If a couple leaves out the unhelpful ingredients mentioned in the first paragraph and adds in all the ingredients suggested including good communication skills, positive intentions, and a good sense of humor; the relationship will be more successful.

It is important to mention here that in some cases couples experience unwanted unconscious patterns in their relationships. When these unconscious patterns arise, the partners may be drawn away from the benefits of the prescribed beneficial ingredients. In these cases, the couple can see a relationship therapist, who can help them bring to light and heal these unwanted patterns as well as help them communicate more effectively. Once these patterns are exposed and healed success resulting from using the beneficial ingredients; presence, availability, trustworthiness, receptiveness, acceptance, respect, forgiveness, patience, understanding, empathy, and compassion will be apparent.

When the partners put this effort into their relationship it will flourish. As an additional benefit or bonus, each partner will most likely notice an improvement in all their interactions; thus the above-mentioned ingredients promotes better relationships of all kinds even with oneself.

A HAPPY MARRIAGE IS NO ACCIDENT

A happy marriage is no accident. As with every other area of life, success in marriage does not happen automatically. The secret to success in any endeavor is planning, and successful planning depends on knowledge. It is only when we have accurate and adeguate information that we can plan for success.

Many of us are willing to spend years in school receiving an education that we believe will prepare us for success in our chosen career or profession. We pursue education because education makes us versatile, and versatility increases our marketability. Increased marketability enhances the likelihood of our success. Rather than leave our success to chance, we plan carefully for it.

There was a time when a person entering the labor force at age 18 or 21 spent his or her entire working life with the same employer. Today it is not at all uncommon for workers to change jobs or employers four or five times or more during their careers. The fact that frequent career changes have become the norm in modern society makes education and knowledge even more important to success.

If we are so careful about planning for career success, why aren't we just as careful about planning for success in marriage? After all, we spend years preparing for a career that may change at any time, yet devote very little time preparing for a relationship that is supposed to last a lifetime. If we are not careful we can end up spending too much time preparing for the wrong things. There is nothing wrong with going to school and getting an education or deliberately planning for success in meeting career goals. The problem is that there are many people who have successful careers but failed marriages because they spent much time learning how to get along with their boss and no time learning how to get along with their spouse. We invest more in preparation to make a living than to live life effectively.

As with any other endeavor in life, success in marriage depends on information and planning. Marriage is an investment, and success is directly proportional to the amount of knowledge and time invested in it. Success is not a gift, but the result of careful and deliberate preparation. Success is directly related to investment: when you invest in time and passion, you will more likely succeed.

No one who hopes to build a new house approaches the project haphazardly. Success in such a venture means buying the right piece of property, securing the services of a qualified architect, and making certain that sufficient financing is available to bring the whole project to completion. It is important to plan for the end before the beginning, to count the cost up front, and try to anticipate the pitfalls and difficulties that will occur along the way.

Jesus emphasized the importance of this kind of advance planning when He said, "Suppose one of you wants to build a tower. Will he not first sit down and estimate the cost to see if he has enough money to complete it? For if he lays the foundation and is not able to finish it, everyone who sees it will ridicule him, saying, 'This fellow began to build and was not able to finish' " (Lk. 14:28-30). Although Jesus was speaking here specifically of counting the cost of following Him as a disciple, His words provide wise counsel for us with regard to any endeavor we undertake. We must plan for success. We must give the same attention to building a home as we do to building the house. Many beautiful houses are not homes.

Building on a Firm Foundation

Anything of a lasting nature is built on a firm and solid foundation, and marriage is no different. Just as a house built on a poor foundation will be blown away in a storm, so marriage is unlikely to survive the tempests of life unless it is firmly established on the bedrock of spiritual principles. Let's consider ten foundation stones upon which to build a happy and successful marriage.

2. Love

Love in marriage is more than just a feeling or an emotion; it is a choice. Love is a decision you make anew every day with regard to your spouse. Whenever you rise up in the morning or lie down at night or go through the affairs of the day, you are choosing continually to love that man or that woman you married.

Understanding that love is a choice will help keep you out of trouble when temptation comes (and it will). Knowing you have made a decision to love your husband or your wife will carry you through those times when he or she has made you angry, or when you see that handsome or attractive coworker at the office. You could have married someone else, but that's not the point. The point is, you made a decision. When you married your spouse, you chose to love and cherish him or her for the rest of your life. That love must be freshened daily.

One of the most important foundation stones for a happy marriage is a sacrificial love for your spouse that you choose to renew daily.

3. Truth

Truth is fundamental in marriage. A marriage that is not based on truth is headed for trouble right away. The greatest and most reliable source of truth is the Bible, which is the Word of God, who is Himself truth and the one who designed and instituted marriage. Every conscientious husband and wife should measure their marriage by the unchanging standard of the principles found in God's Word.

Truthfulness between husband and wife is an indispensable part of a successful marriage. No one's interests are served if spouses are not honest with each other. Honesty, tempered and seasoned with love, fosters an environment of trust.

4. Trust

Trust is closely related to truth. If a husband and wife want their marriage to be happy and successful, they must be able to trust each other implicitly. Nothing damages a marriage more than broken trust. It's hard to grow and prosper in an atmosphere of bitterness, resentment, and suspicion.

That is why both partners should take great care to ensure that they do not say or do anything to give each other any reason to doubt or distrust them. Trust enables a husband and wife to enjoy a relationship characterized by openness and transparency, with no secrets or "locked rooms" that are kept off-limits to each other. Trust is also an essential element of commitment.

5. Commitment

Commitment is a frightening word to many people in our society today. They are afraid of being locked in or tied down to any kind of a long-term arrangement. That is one reason why many marriages do not last. A man and a woman approach the marriage altar and exchange their vows but are just going through the motions, giving only lip service to commitment. Their idea of marriage is to hang together until the going gets rough, and then they can split. If their marriage "works," okay, and if it doesn't, oh well. Few people who marry plan for their marriages to fail, but neither do they specifically plan for success. Those who do not plan for success are virtually guaranteed to fail.

Commitment is the lifeblood of a marriage. Part of our problem is that we do not understand the nature of a covenant. Marriage is a "blood covenant" of sorts and, like the blood covenants of old, it lasts a lifetime. A blood covenant was neither entered into nor broken lightly. Violation of a blood covenant brought serious consequences. Marriage involves just as serious a commitment. It is, first of all, a commitment to the institution of marriage and, second, an exclusive commitment to that person we have chosen to love and cherish for life.

6. **Respect**

Any healthy relationship, marriage included, must be built on mutual respect. To respect someone means to esteem that person, to consider him or her worthy of high regard. Wives should respect their husbands and husbands should respect their wives. One reason why so many marriages are in trouble is because the husband has never learned to regard his wife with proper respect. Many men grow up to regard women as little more than sex objects to be possessed and used at will. Never learning any different, they carry this same ignorant viewpoint into marriage.

God created man—male and female—in His own image. He created them equal in every significant way. Husbands and wives who see each other as made in God's image will never have any problems with respect. Whoever desires respect must show respect to others and live in a manner worthy of respect. Anyone who would be respected must be respectable.

7. Submission

Healthy marriages are built not only on mutual respect but also on mutual submission. We hear so often that wives are supposed to submit to their husbands that we forget that submission goes both ways. "Submit to one another out of reverence for Christ. Wives, submit to your husbands as to the Lord...Husbands, love your wives, just as Christ loved the church and gave Himself up for her" (Eph. 5:21-22,25). Jesus' giving Himself up in death out of love for His Church was the ultimate act of submission. Ephesians 5:25 says that husbands are supposed to love their wives in that same way, a love characterized by sacrificial, self-giving submission.

Properly understood, there is nothing demeaning about submission. It is chosen freely, not imposed from without. Essentially, submission is the willingness to give up our right to ourselves, to freely surrender our insistence on having our own way all the time. Submission means putting the needs, rights, and welfare of another person ahead of our own. A marriage built on this kind of submission will grow healthy, strong, and fulfilling.

8. Knowledge

It would be almost impossible to over-emphasize the importance of knowledge as a firm foundation for marriage. Many marriages struggle or fail because of lack of knowledge. Couples enter married life with no clue as to what marriage is or is not. They carry unrealistic and unreasonable expectations of themselves, their spouses, and their relationship as a whole.

This is why a period of courtship and engagement is so important and why premarital counseling is indispensable. Couples considering marriage need time to get to know one another. They need time to talk about their dreams, their desires, and their expectations. They need time to study and learn the spiritual foundations and principles for marriage that God has given in His Word. With all the resources that are currently available, and because so much is at stake, there is no excuse today for marital ignorance or illiteracy.

9. Faithfulness

Faithfulness is closely related to commitment and also has a lot to do with trust. When we speak of faithfulness in marriage, we most often have sexual relations in mind. Faithful partners will be true, reserving sexual expression exclusively for each other. This is why many married couples who were sexually active before marriage often have trouble in their relationships. The basic element of faithfulness is missing. Even if they have pledged to be faithful to each other, there is always that shadow of doubt. It doesn't take much for that shadow to become a dark storm cloud looming over everything.

Marital faithfulness involves more than just sexual fidelity. Being faithful to your wife also means defending her and affirming her beauty, intelligence, and integrity at all times, particularly before other people. Faithfulness to your husband means sticking up for him, always building him up and never tearing him down. Marital fidelity means that your spouse's health, happiness, security, and welfare take a higher place in your life than anything else except your own relationship with the Lord.

10. Patience

Patience is another essential foundation stone for building a successful and happy marriage. Why? Marriage brings together two totally different people with different experiences, different backgrounds, different temperaments, different likes and dislikes, and sometimes even different cultures. Because of these differences, both partners will have to make major adjustments in their lives and attitudes if their marriage is to succeed. Some bumps and bruises along the way are inevitable. She may wear her hair in a way he doesn't like. He may drive her up the wall with his habit of leaving his dirty clothes lying around everywhere. They may have a conflict regarding expectations, money management, use of leisure time, sex, parenting—any number of things. The critical key in dealing with conflict and adjusting to differences is patience. Both partners will need truckloads of it!

11. Financial stability

Financial stability is one of the most often overlooked foundation stones of marriage. Many young couples who are planning to marry give little thought to the importance of entering marriage with a well-established financial base. I cannot count the number of times I have seen this for myself.

A young couple comes to me and says,

"We would like to get married."

"Are either of you working?" "No."

"Then how do you expect to make it?"

"We're in love. We'll make it. Love will find a way."

Love is certainly important, even critical, but let's be practical. Love won't pay the rent or put food on the table. Adjusting to married life is difficult and challenging enough on its own. The last thing a couple need is to go into the marriage with a lot of minus. Financial instability is one of the biggest minuses of all. If you're having money problems before you are married, what makes you think they will go away after you are married?

The time to think about finances is before the wedding—long before. A couple should discuss the matter frankly and honestly and have a clear financial plan in place before they take their vows. There should be a steady and dependable source of income. At the very least, the man should have steady employment. No woman, even if she has her own career and plans to continue working, should marry a man who does not have a job. If she does, she will most likely end up supporting him, rather than the other way around.

Financial difficulty is one of the main causes of marital failure. Never underestimate the importance of financial stability to a successful marriage.

Checking Your "Marriage Ability" Traits

In addition to these foundation stones, there are several "marriage ability" traits we should consider —qualities of personality and character that will enhance the building of a strong marriage. Check these out and see where you stand. I have listed seven.

Adaptability.

This is simply the ability to adapt to changing conditions. No matter how carefully we prepare for marriage, we cannot predict everything. Unexpected situations will pop up with annoying frequency, forcing us to change our plans. Just the fact of two completely different people coming together as one will inevitably call for flexibility. Be adaptable. Expect the unexpected. Consider it as an opportunity to grow, to move in a direction you might never have thought of otherwise.

Ability to work through problems.
This is not the same as solving problems. Some problems cannot be solved, but married couples need the ability to identify and analyze problems, propose and choose a possible solution, and follow it through. They will be able to solve most problems this way and will learn to work around the ones they can't solve. The important thing is being committed to deal with problems, not walk away from them.

Ability to give and receive love.
This is not as easy as it sounds, particularly for most men. Giving and receiving love comes more naturally to women. Men, on the other hand, have been taught in society that being manly or "macho" means not showing their sensitive side openly. As a result, many men have trouble expressing their true

feelings. Marriage is a constant give-and-take, and this includes expression of love.

Emotional stability.

This means being able to control our emotions and not let them run away from us. It means bridling our temper and not making excuses for immature emotional outbursts. Occasional loss of control is human but a pattern of it reveals a deeper problem. Anyone who constantly flies off the handle then says, "I can't help myself," is not being honest. If that is truly the case, then that person needs professional help. Usually, however, it is not a matter of being unable, but of being unwilling. Emotional stability means being willing and able to accept responsibility for our feelings, words, and actions.

Ability to communicate.

True communication is not easy and happens rarely. Communication is the ability to ensure that people understand not only what you say but also what you mean. It is also the ability to listen to and understand others. Developing both of these aspects of communication takes a lot of time, patience, and hard work.

Similarities between the couples themselves.
Any marriage involves the joining of two totally different people, but there should be some distinct similarities as well: common interests, common hobbies, a common faith, or similar political views for example. There needs to be some common meeting ground between the two.

Similar family background.
Although this is not a highly critical factor—people of distinctly different backgrounds build successful marriages every day—similar family background is always helpful. A couple should enter marriage with all the advantages or "pluses" that they can, and similarity of family background is definitely a "plus."

As important as they are, foundation stones alone are incomplete. They merely form the base upon which the completed structure must be built. The foundation stones of love, truth, trust, commitment, respect, submission, knowledge, faithfulness, patience, and financial stability are not ends in themselves. Rather they are bases upon which to build and display the beautiful jewel that we call marriage—a fusion of two distinct persons into one flesh, soul, and spirit. Success and happiness are no accident, but the result and reward of deliberate planning, diligent pursuit, and patient growth.

GETTING MARRIED

There are many reasons for marriage. Some people get married because they can't stand watching television alone. Others marry because of a need for sexual expression. Some get married because they're afraid they'll have no one to take care of them when they're old and feeble. Others get married for financial security. Some choose marriage because it's the most acceptable form for having and raising children. Some wed because of parental and social conditioning that says it is the thing to do. Yet, others marry to balance past experiences. And some even marry for love.

In many of those situations, people seldom admit to themselves or to their spouse their real reasons for marrying. They may marry under the banner of love, but not for the substance. Some remain married for many years with such unspoken thoughts as "is that all there is?" And others may separate with, "If that's all there is, I don't want it."

I often suggest to couples who have recently met that they should not be in a hurry to marry. I suggest they spend time getting to know each other. How long? A minimum of six months and I encourage two years. In the first six months, the two usually love each other with such infatuation that they automatically cooperate, accept, love, flow, participate, accommodate, nurture, resolve, and share.

In two years, however, some people start expressing negatively, in terms of competing, ignoring, and rejecting. That's the bad news. The good news is that if the couple has been going together for two years, it is easier to conclude the relationship, choosing not to participate in the negativity, and learning what they can from the relationship as they go on their way.

I know couples who have seen an attorney before they married in order to work out a contract that defined financial and other elements of their intended relationship, including a detailed account of what would happen in the event of a divorce. Although that may be very practical, it certainly isn't very romantic. But then, does it have to be?

My point of view is that if a couple has to make a legal agreement stipulating conditions for a divorce before they are married, why get married? My guideline is, when in doubt, don't do, or when in doubt, talk it out. Marriage, from the point of view of unconditional loving, is difficult enough in a conditioned world. If people get married for the wrong reasons, they are likely to get divorced for the right reasons.

Some people take romance to the extreme and marry thinking that they and their mate are and will always be everything to each other. That's a fallacy. Trying to work a marriage on that everything-to-each-other basis is like trying to live in a state of perfection in an imperfect situation. That isn't the way things are designed on this perfectly imperfect planet. What the marriage is based on will most likely determine the loving or lack of loving expressed, as well as the duration of the relationship.

If a marriage is based only upon the love of sex, it will not last very long—perhaps a year. If, in addition to the sexual expression, each one enjoys the physicality of the other person, that may add a few years to the relationship. But a marriage based primarily on looking at and making love to each other is limited in terms of time and expression.

Then there are marriages based on emotions. Part of this can be staying married for the sake of the children, and after the children are gone, there can often be divorce. An emotionally based marriage will last longer if it includes mental love. What does a couple do after the children are gone and they feel less desire for the sexual expression? A marriage including mental love, where a couple loves to talk and share, can last a lifetime.

If you get married because you are in love, then know that you can just as easily be out of love. If you get married because you love your mate for what he or she will do, then you may not love them if they don't do what you want or expect. But if you marry simply because you love the other person and it doesn't matter what they do, then that is the marriage that can endure and be enjoyed throughout all experiences for a lifetime.

In those marriages where the unconditional, spiritual love is present, total love on all levels is likely, including a harmonious balance of the mental, emotional, physical, and sexual expressions. You live together in a natural state of living love. This is closest to the happily-ever-after fantasy.

TOWARDS MAKING THE RIGHT CHOICE OF WHO TO MARRY

Quite often, the success of our marriage to a large extent depends on the type of person we choose as our marriage partner. That is why making the right choice of who to marry is one of the uphill tasks of some young men.

Some couples whose marriages had failed, some claimed that the major reason for the failure was because they made the wrong choice of who they married.

The above is a pointer to show that the success or failure of our marriage is determined by the choice of the man or woman we married. During marriage seminars, one of the questions that are always in the lips of some young men and eligible bachelors is "how do they know the right person to marry?"

The normal answer I usually give to them is that they should try and be the right person. This is because like attract like and it is said that birds of the same feather flocks together. That is to say, it is our person that determines if a man or woman will be compatible with us or not. You can't just marry anybody because not everybody will be compatible with you.

So you should try to be the right person if you wish to get the right person to marry: This is the first step in choosing the right person to marry as a wife or husband. If you are not the right person, even if you marry the right person, your marriage may never work. For instance, what do you say of a very lazy man but wish to marry a very hard working woman?

You must have adequate knowledge of who you really are: It is having adequate and true knowledge of yourself, who you really are that guides you to choose the kind of person you need as a wife or husband.

If you don't know who you are, you may not be able to know the kind of person you need as a husband or wife. It is the knowledge of who you are that enables you to determine the kind of person you need as a wife or husband that will be compatible with you.

You should define your choice of the kind of woman or man you want as a husband or wife:

Having the right knowledge of who you are, the next step is to define your choice. It is said that if you don't know what you are looking for, it will be likely that you will never know when you find it.

A look at what happened in the book of Genesis 24: 12 -22 clearly show the need to have a mental picture of the kind of woman you want as a wife. It is that picture that you pray to God about. In that passage above, the oldest servant of Abraham who went to take a wife for Isaac made a prayer based on the kind of woman he wants for Isaac: Then he said, "O LORD God of my master Abraham, please give me success this day, and show kindness to my master Abraham.

He said in verses 13 -14 "Behold, here I stand by the well of water, and the daughters of the men of the city are coming out to draw water. "Now let it be that the young woman to whom I say, 'Please let down your pitcher that I may drink,' and she says, 'Drink, and I will also give your camels a drink' - let her be the one You have appointed for Your servant Isaac. And by this, I will know that You have shown kindness to my master."

Also in verses 15-17 And it happened before he had finished speaking, that behold, Rebekah, who was born to Bethuel, son of Milcah, the wife of Nahor, Abraham's brother, came out with her pitcher on her shoulder.

Now the young woman was very beautiful to behold, a virgin; no man had known her. And she went down to the well, filled her pitcher, and came up. And the servant ran to meet her and said, "Please let me drink a little water from your pitcher."

In verses 18-22 So she said, "Drink, my lord." Then she quickly let her pitcher down to her hand and gave him a drink. And when she had finished giving him a drink, she said, "I will draw water for your camels also, until they have finished drinking." Then she quickly emptied her pitcher into the trough, ran back to the well to draw water, and drew for all his camels.

And the man, wondering at her, remained silent so as to know whether the LORD had made his journey prosperous or not. So it was when the camels had finished drinking, that the man took a golden nose ring weighing half a shekel, and two bracelets for her wrists weighing ten shekels of gold,

In defining your choice, I counsel young men that they should pay attention to who they are and where they are going rather than where they are presently.

Also, ladies, you should consider a man for marriage not based on his present position or situation but on whom he really is and his future prospect in life.

Again, in defining your choice of the kind of person you wish to marry, you should try and be realistic and very objective in your choice. To guide you, you should ask and answer the following questions:

The person I desire to marry, will that person equally desire and accept to marry me?

Will I be proud of that person I wish and desire to marry and will that person accept and equally be proud of me?

Will I be proud to be the father or mother of his or her children and will he or she be proud of me being the father or mother of his or her children?

I counsel young men and women, you should really marry the person you are proud of both now and in the future. If you marry the person you are not proud of, in the future, you may start to compare him or her with other men or women in town and that leads to a crash of marriages.

Again, in defining the kind of person you need as a wife or husband, you need to take into consideration certain factors such as character, the person's background, beauty and the social class which he or she belongs to among other things. I said this because you need to choose a person who has a positive contribution to make in your life rather than reduce it.

Also as a man, you should endeavor to choose a woman you really love, a woman who you feel will compliment you and be submissive to you. And as a woman, never marry a man who you are not sure of his love for you and a man you feel that you would not respect and be submissive to.

Also, in making the right choice of who to marry, you must consider a person who is ready and willing to compromise for the sake of his or her marriage. If you observe some failed marriages, one of the reasons the couples cite as the cause of their marriage failure is "irreconcilable differences".

If you choose a man or woman that is selfish and always insist on having his or her way in every issue, your marriage will never last as this will be a wrong choice. If you happen to marry such a person, you will either endure the marriage or you will end up as well with the problem of "irreconcilable differences".

RULES FOR FINDING LOVE

- **Be Yourself**

Isn't it so tempting to reinvent yourself when you meet somebody new who you really like—try and be who you think they are looking for? You could become sophisticated, or maybe strong, silent, and mysterious. At the very least, you could stop embarrassing yourself by making jokes at inappropriate moments or being pathetic when dealing with problems.

Actually, no you couldn't. You might manage it for an evening or two, or even a month or two, but it's going to be tough keeping it up forever. And if you think this person is the one—you know, the one— then you might be spending the next half century or so with them. Just imagine, 50 years of pretending to be sophisticated or suppressing your natural sense of humor.

That's not going to happen, is it? And would you actually want a lifetime of lurking behind some sham personality you've created? Imagine how that would be, unable ever to let on that this wasn't really you at all, for fear of losing them. Suppose they find out in a few weeks or months or years, when you finally crack? They're not going to be very impressed.

Let's be clear. I'm not saying you shouldn't try to turn over the occasional new leaf or improve yourself a bit. We should all be doing that all the time, and not only in our love life. Sure, you can try to be a bit more organized, or less negative. Changing your behavior is all fine and good. This Rule is about changing your basic personality. That will NOT work, and you'll tie yourself in knots trying to do it convincingly.

So be you. Might as well get it all out in the open now—if it's not who they're looking for, at least you won't get in too deep before they find out. And you know what? Maybe they don't actually like sophisticated. Perhaps strong silent types don't do it for them. Maybe they'll love your upfront sense of humor. Perhaps they want to be with someone who needs a bit of looking after.

You see, if you fake it, you'll attract someone who belongs with a person that isn't you. And how will that help? Somewhere out there is someone who wants exactly the kind of person you are, complete with all the flaws and failings you come with. And I'll tell you something else—they won't even see them as flaws and failings. They'll see them as part of your unique charm. And they'll be right.

- **Get Over It Before You Get on with It**

We all get battered and bruised by life, that's inevitable. Some of us come off worse than others. Of course, it's the scars that give us character, so they're not all bad in the long run. In the short term, we may need to recover before we re-enter the fray.

If your last relationship or two has left you a bit of an emotional wreck, it's better to repair the damage before you start looking for a new lover and partner. Otherwise you won't be able to show them the real you, and you won't be able to focus on them if you're still preoccupied with yourself.

If you make a mistake with your new relationship (and it happens to us all), you could end up more bruised than when you started. Even if you did manage to find someone truly caring and loving, both of you could suffer because one of you wasn't ready yet to launch into a relationship.

I have a friend who came out of one relationship an emotional wreck. Then she met a man who was lovely—kind, nurturing, and protective. Just what she thought she needed. Over the next couple of years he looked after her until she was a strong, independent woman again. And what happened? It completely killed their relationship. She wasn't the woman he'd fallen in love with any more. Lots of men go for strong, independent women, but he wasn't one of them. He liked women who were fragile and needed looking after.

And that's the danger. Even if you find the perfect partner, they're only ideal for who you are right now, and that's not who you'll be after you recover —the person you really are underneath. I'm not saying these relationships can never work, but it's very, very rare.

So do yourself a favor. Go away and hide somewhere while you lick your wounds. Enjoy your friends and your family, and wait until you've recovered before you start looking for a new partner. And when you do, try to pick someone whose scars are relatively well-healed, too— because this works the other way as well. In this way you both see each other as you trully are, and start your relationship the way you want to continue it.

• **Choose Someone Who Makes You Laugh**

I nearly put this Rule first because I think it is the most important thing of all in a relationship. If you choose your partner for their looks, their status, even the rest of their personality, you could eventually regret it. Anyway, lots of those things can get lost along the way. Even personality traits can change—a confident person can be shattered by an emotional trauma, a patient person can become irritable and frustrated through illness or pain.

A sense of humor will last you long after everything else has gone. When you're both sitting there in your rocking chairs, decades after retirement and the kids have long since grown up, it may be all you have left. If it is, it will be enough.

Laughter is worth its weight in gold. A sense of humor is a very personal thing, and some people just make us laugh more than others. When you find the person who really makes you laugh more than anyone else, marry them. That's my advice. You're almost guaranteed to admire them more, because anyone who makes you laugh will be hugely attractive—even if they're not physically what you'd been anticipating.

Okay, I'm being a little extreme, but only slightly. Personally I married the person who made me laugh more than anyone else, and it was absolutely the right thing to do. Maybe you'll prefer to go for the second or third funniest person you meet. Just don't compromise on the sense of humor, because it really is the top priority.

You don't just want someone who makes you laugh generally, although that's essential. The best thing of all is to find someone who can make you laugh at yourself. That will get you through life more smoothly than anything.

I have a friend whose wife died a few years ago, and he says that one of the things he misses most is being able to laugh at himself. He hadn't realized how much she helped him to do that or how essential it was to his happiness. He says he takes himself far too seriously these days and gets stressed about things that she would have gotten him to laugh off.

So next time you meet someone with gorgeous legs, sexy eyes, or a cute smile, don't be seduced right away. See if they can first tickle you without touching.

- **You Won't Be Happy with a Partner Until You Can Be Happy on Your Own**

I knew a woman who was always in a relationship. You know the kind—maybe you're the same—the moment one relationship ended, another started. I asked her once why this was, and she told me that she didn't like being on her own so she made sure it never happened. When I got to know her well, she was with a man who was perfectly decent but who just didn't give her the love she deserved. Why did she put up with it, I asked her. She patiently explained that she had no choice, because the alternative was being on her own, and she couldn't cope with that option.

In the end, things got really bad and he left. She braced herself for the breakdown she knew would follow. I saw her a month or so later and asked how she was coping. She told me, "Fine, at the moment.

I thought I would have fallen to pieces by now, but it's obviously taking longer to happen than I expected."

I think it was six months before it finally dawned on her that she wasn't actually going to break down at all. Three months later, she met a lovely guy who wanted to get serious and move in together, but she resisted. She was having too much fun being on her own.

The point of this story is that she stayed in relationships that weren't good and put up with flak she didn't deserve, out of fear of being on her own. After she knew that she was happy on her own, she set her standards much higher and wouldn't put up with second best. She didn't have to. After all, what was the worst that could happen? Well, she could end up back on her own again—but that wasn't a problem any more.

So the moral of this story is that you need to learn to be happy and secure on your own. That way, you'll never stay in a bad situation for fear of being left alone. If it's not working out, you can simply leave. Far too many people stay in unhappy relationships because they're scared to be alone. Rules players learn to enjoy living alone so that when they do choose to throw in their lot with a new partner, it's for the right reasons.

After you've mastered this, you'll only ever live with anyone else because you love them and they make you happy. Being alone is great, but being with them is even better. If that stops being the case, you're free to leave.

• You'll Know Them When You Meet Them

To be quite honest, I'm not sure this is entirely true. Some people do know the instant they meet their future partner that this is the person they've been looking for all their life. But it doesn't work like that for everyone.

The real rule is that if you're not sure if this is the right one, don't take a gamble on it. If they are the right one, you will know it, even if it takes a bit of time. In other words, if it's right you will be sure either straight away, or a bit later but you will know.

If you're absolutely sure this is the right person the moment you lock eyes on them, you're very lucky. (Unless it happens to you every time, in which case you need to stop kidding yourself.) The important thing is not to commit yourself until you're certain. How many divorced people have you heard say, "Do you know, even on my wedding day I was wondering if I was doing the right thing."

Well, I can tell you. If you're still wondering about it on your wedding day, you are not doing the right thing. You are making a big mistake. Marriage and/or kids are tough enough when you are sure you are with the right person. It's lunacy to enter into it without being certain.

If you aren't sure right at the beginning, that's normal. It may take weeks, months, or even years to be sure, especially if you're of a naturally doubtful persuasion. That's all fine. It's just that until you are sure, you shouldn't be making a permanent commitment.

Your new partner, of course, may be sure sooner than you are. We're all different. But don't allow them to pressure you into making a decision before you're ready. It's understandable that they want you to commit yourself—you're a wonderful person, why wouldn't they want to be with you? But no one will benefit if you make the wrong decision.

If this is really the right person for you to spend your life with, you won't be thinking, "I don't know.

Is it me? I'm just not sure if this is right." You'll be thinking, "Yes, yes, yes, let's get on with it!" If you're not thinking that, you're not ready to commit yourself.

THERE'S GOING TO BE SOME CHANGES MADE

When couples don't have enough experience or will power to go for the positive, they often have won't-power and point out all the things that are supposedly wrong with the other person.

It can get downright nasty, to the point of one saying, "If I had known you were like that, I wouldn't have married you." The honest response might be, "I knew that which is why I didn't let you know." Then each of them is faced with the challenge of loving the other enough (with all that they do know) to look at the imperfections through the eyes of love.

Some people may stick to the traditional struggle: "I'll love you only if you change." If the response is, "I won't change until you change," the couple may be stuck with that. Another response might be, "Why must I change? Why can't I just have that imperfection, and we continue to relate in loving anyway?" The choice, then, is to go for that or to stay stuck in an emotional reaction of "because when you do that, it makes me sick."

It could be time for you to get in touch with that sick feeling and see if it has as much to do with the other person as it does with cultural conditioning that is giving birth to judgment. In other words, your past may be clouding your present. Imperfections don't always have to be regarded as bad news. The good news is that human frailties and imperfections are often shared only when a person relaxes enough not to edit their thoughts, habits, or feelings.

For example, imagine having the courage to admit, "You're the only one who can hurt me, and you're the only one I've ever trusted enough to show these things. I know I need help, but you want me to change before I know what I'm dealing with and how to change it. You're ready to walk out the door before I've even begun to look at a habit I developed long before I met you. Can't we sit and look at it?

Maybe I can change it if I know what I'm going to change. Not change just to please you, but change the formula that caused it. And that takes some looking, some investigation, some knowing that lets me get in touch with it."

It is the inability to get in touch with a habitual response that makes it so difficult to change. It's like trying to open a combination lock without turning the dial. No matter how much you theorize, until you actually get in there and start experimenting to find out what the process is, you can't come close to unlocking the habit.

In loving—real loving, which is unconditional—you can assist your lover rather than criticize or issue ultimatums. Rather than a change-or-else attitude, a supportive approach of loving no matter what will encourage adjustments.

What do you think will be produced by the attitude of, "I'm going to marry you, but you have to change?" Probably not change. Or if there is change, it may be accompanied by resentment because the change came about as a result of intimidation or coercion. If you issue a change-or-else ultimatum, at best you may end up with a change and an "or else"— the "or else" being resentment.

You might think, "Well, if I don't demand the change, I'm stuck with the behavior that makes me crazy." Again, maybe it's your responsibility to get in touch with what makes you crazy. "My spouse's behavior" may be your immediate response, but I would bet that you have that "get crazy" button pushed and set off by people other than just your spouse. Get in touch with it. It's your button that is being pushed. Instead of trying to change the button pushers so quickly, how about removing the button itself or changing your response when the button is pushed?

You can always leave your loved one in your righteous indignation. This will leave you open to find another person to love, who will most likely test and bless you with even greater imperfections that push the it-makes-me-crazy button harder and more often. If this happens, you're likely to leave that relationship even quicker than the previous one.

It's important for your relationship that you do not treat your mate's problem as more important than your mate. I don't care what the nature of the problem is. Problems are to be dealt with but don't make the mistake of thinking that the problems are your husband or your wife. Your loved one is bigger than the problem. You can assist your mate in avoiding inappropriate behavior as long as you communicate that you love him or her more than the issue of concern.

I know of one husband who experiences great stress at work and needs time to unwind when he comes home. Sometimes, before he has had sufficient time to relax, his wife or his children may demand some attention that he's not yet ready to give. He often responds irritably, to the point of anger and impatience. His wife and children know him, and they usually just laugh. "That's Daddy. Give him 15 more minutes, rub his shoulders, and he'll be back to normal." You see, you don't always have to react to someone's frailty or even demand that they change. Some can even be observed, tolerated, and laughed with if you will.

SEXUAL FIDELITY, FANTASIES, AND FREQUENCY

Inherent in most committed relationships is the understanding that each of you will have sex only with the other. If this is not clear in each of your minds and hearts, please be sure to talk about it.

When the sexual expression is a loving, intimate, physical gesture of affection, it will normally contribute loving, positive energy to a couple. If there is deceit involved in that area, however, negativity can be received into your being, and the natural energy can be depleted. Deceit in the sexual area can cause distress, disease, and divorce.

I encourage couples to be honest with each other in sharing their intent regarding sexual fidelity and in living up to their agreement; if the agreement is changed on either side, the partner is to be notified right away.

Actually, if you have come to a reluctant agreement in bartering, give-and-take sessions, you might want to take a good, long, hard look at your relationship. If you feel that making love only to your mate is a restriction, you may be involved in the wrong kind of relationship. Perhaps it might be better if you two were not together, because if you are involved in a loving, committed relationship, the natural, preferred expression is fidelity. The sexual expression of love, shared only between two committed lovers, is what making love is all about. Anything less is distracting; anything more can be harmful.

It doesn't matter all that much if you feel lust when you see an attractive man or woman other than your mate. What does matter is whether you let this lust run you; it matters what you're going to do with it when it does appear.

Some people choose to have an affair with that other person, justifying it by saying they're getting lust out of their system. Maybe so, but they may also be getting into their system other things: guilt, remorse, despair, feelings of betrayal, and even degradation.

That hell which is part of betrayal fulfills the saying "your sins have found you out," because your guilt may punish you more than the mere sexual act. You may be further ahead not to give in to lust under any rationale. If you do choose it, then do it knowingly, accepting all that comes with it and owning your behavior.

It's a matter of learning discipline and self-control instead of giving in to a primal lust that disappears a mini-second after the act and keeps reemerging again and again and again because it can never be satisfied. Being a slave to an unquenchable thirst is not a very smart way to live.

There are some people who think they can get away with it. They're convinced that if they take such care that their mate does not discover them, no one will be the wiser and no one will be hurt. There is always a knower. It's in yourself, certainly, and your body, emotions, and life experiences will reflect such a betrayal no matter what rationale you offer.

There is also your perceptive mate. He or she may not know specifically what has happened, but there very well might be some intuitive recording that may root deeply as separation in your relationship. Perhaps someday this root may spring forth and grow into something like a divorce when your mate says, "I found another lover." It's called "chickens come home to roost" or "as you sow, so shall you reap."

If you already know that making love and later falling asleep with your mate is the only way to go, you have a good start on a loving, lasting relationship.

A husband or wife may sometimes fantasize another person in their arms as they are making love to their mate. Perhaps without knowing it, the one who is fantasizing is pushing the other away. If you do this, you may be either making love because of pressure and expectations—thus creating the fantasy in order to perform—or having sex more often than you'd prefer. You may be having sex, rather than making love, to prove yourself because of unconscious insecurity about your gender or relationship.

If you are not sexually stimulated by the person who is present at the moment, I encourage you not to create a fantasy in order to justify and fulfill the act. The person—your lover, your wife, or your husband—is the one who is present, and both of you deserve all of your attention (physical, emotional, mental, imaginative, and spiritual) during the highly charged sexual expression.

Your lover is a pearl of great price. Don't use sex only as "casual recreation" with someone so precious. Instead, you can use sex as one form of intimacy and sharing. In that context, a recharging and oneness evolve as each of you becomes secure with the other and with yourselves as a couple. That is the most comfortable form of togetherness.

You don't have to use sexual intercourse in order to be sexual, sensual, or romantic. You can share a shower or a massage, lie with each other and listen to music that opens the heart, cuddle, and fall asleep. That, too, is romance.

When couples shifts from the courting period to marriage, the sexual expression often changes, becoming less romantic, less charged, and usually less frequent. Don't worry or judge yourself or your partner if this occurs. It is part of the qualitative and quantitative change that often takes place with increased physical proximity and a committed relationship. There are seldom concerns of "will she?" or "is he?" Part of the built-in condition of your marriage is an expectation that the sexual expression will be available.

Let the change be all right. Let the fact that you may romance each other differently be permissible. That is not to say that you should be inconsiderate or mechanical. No. Never forget that the sexual expression is called lovemaking. Make sure that no matter how, where, or when, you are making love to and with your mate.

Many animals have mating periods, and some people say that this is not the case with human beings. I'm not so sure about that. In my observation and counselings with couples who have been married from 2 to 20 years, I have found that people do go through sexual cycles.

There seem to be recurring periods when individual men and women are not as sexually assertive or not as receptive to the sexual act. This is not to say that the loving diminishes. Not at all. It is just part of nature's cycle that the expression is not always on "high." You don't need to judge or feel guilty about this. Just become aware of your own particular rhythm and share your awareness with your mate.

One of the worst things a couple can do is go to bed with pressure and sleep with unresolved discomfort. If the man reaches out and the woman says "not tonight, honey" often enough and without a heart-to-heart discussion, the man may stop reaching out to her, and eventually he may go reach out outside of the house. The same thing holds if a woman wants to make love and the man doesn't want to turn off the eleven o'clock news on TV. If the man does that often enough, his wife may be the one making the news.

I suggest that you share lovingly, candidly, and intimately. Know that it is not only all right, but it is more usual than people will admit, that there are high and low sexual cycles. If such is the case for you on occasion, you can share this with your partner: "Honey, I'm crazy in love with you, and I'm going through a period where I just want to fall asleep holding you. I don't know what it is, but I love you and I just don't feel like sex. It may just be a cycle, and it has nothing to do with the fact that I deeply love you."

That kind of loving honesty makes it much easier for a man or a woman to handle sexual cycles. In the sharing, there is no feeling of rejection, blame, or guilt. Then, indeed, you can both go to sleep lovingly, knowing that sexual cycles are normal— not good or bad, but just part of nature.

SUCCESS-FULL MARRIAGE

Most people would probably say that a successful marriage is based on unconditional loving. The truth is, however, that people usually don't marry because of unconditional loving; they marry for conditioned loving. Conditions are presented to each other, including that they love one another unconditionally, based upon conditions. They often demand that the other person fill that empty, lonely, insecure space inside of them, and the person simply doesn't know how to do that. No one knows how to fill up anybody else regardless of all the romantic songs and movies. In fact, very few know how to fill themselves up.

Rather than attempt to be unconditionally loving 100 percent of the time and demand that your lover is in a similar state "or else," I suggest that each of you choose the experience that exists at the moment. By choosing, I mean accepting what is going on with no judgment, blame, or ultimatum.

If something is bothering you about his or her behavior, you can change your focus rather than get upset. Doing this requires commitment and inner discipline. In fact, marriage, in order to be successful, requires 100 percent commitment to loving—commitment, not necessarily accomplishment. In other words, if your partner sometimes exhibits less-than-loving behavior, don't beat them over the head with, "But you agreed to 100 percent commitment!"

Commitment really means that you both go for 100 percent loving. Don't expect perfection because it may not be available, and the paradox is that you still go for it. The best you'll end up with is excellence, and excellence in love is almost totally fulfilling.

What will eliminate the "almost" and actually bring fulfillment is the other elements necessary to a successful relationship: total acceptance of the other. Accepting all the positive attributes is easy. How about accepting human frailties, without judgment, resentment, or disappointment? (Judgment, by the way, is an attempt to get people to think you are perfect. When someone is perfect, the implication is that they have the right to judge.

Actually, however, in the perfected state, there is no judgment because you can see that all is, indeed, perfect.)

In any situation, get beyond the words to the heart because if the heart is not heard, no words can really help. Once into the heart of yours and your lover's, then you can give and receive, lift and be lifted. If you're not loving and caring for each other, there is really no need to be together.

You can go through junk and disagreements together, as long as you are both committed to going through and getting through the junk, together. The more you both do that, the quiker you will get through it until, ultimately, that junkyard will be history, a historical frame of reference for yourself and others. In order to make your marriage work, first, go within yourself and make a secure and safe place for each of you.

Safety and security are products accompanied by liberal doses of the following ingredients: compassion, acceptance, humor, and a double helping of love.

To make a marriage work, you also have to continue to get married, every day. In fact, it might be called "marriage," an ongoing activity of nourishing and caring for each other.

I know two people very much in love. After observing them for three years, I've seen that their love is more joyful and humorous than ever before. Why? Because they are married. They keep the relationship alive by acts that are accepting and nourishing. Here is an example of something that happened to them recently:

One day, while driving to a movie, the man felt that his wife was separating from him. It wasn't anything she said or did, but when you are deeply in love with a person, you can often intuit something without obvious indications. He asked his wife, "Is anything wrong? " She said, "No, I'm just quiet."

When they parked the car he still felt the separation. Again he said, "Are you sure everything's all right?" She said, "Yes, I just need to be alone for a little while." His initial reaction was anger, tension, and all those other emotional-hurt buttons. After all, they had planned to go to a movie and to have a pizza and a wonderful day together. Yet here she was, separating.

He was aware of his emotions starting to rise but chose not to give energy to those feelings and thoughts. He just said, "How long do you want to be alone?" She said, "About 15 or 20 minutes." He said, "Okay. The movie doesn't start for 30 minutes. I'll meet you in front of the theater in 20 minutes." And he left her in the car.

The woman remained in the car, spending time alone with herself. She didn't understand what was going on, nor did she judge it. She simply gave herself permission to be with her thoughts, her feelings, and whatever else came up. She sat there and indulged in just being, a beautiful gift.

As for him, while walking he went through moments of experiencing rejection, anger, and isolation. Then he got distracted from those emotions by people-watching and window shopping, and he started to enjoy being alone. Eventually, he found himself in front of a flower store. "What the heck," he thought, "so she needs to be alone. I'm having a great time, and I'm crazy about her, so I'm going to surprise her with flowers."

That's just what he did. He bought her three roses, one white, one yellow, and one purple, and managed to put them in his back pocket, so when he saw her she wouldn't immediately see the flowers.

She was waiting for him in front of the theater, having done whatever it was she needed to do to balance herself. She was now ready to be with him, and she hugged him. Then she felt something sticking out of his back pocket. The discovery of his loving gift of flowers allowed them both to laugh and enjoy as they went into the theater, and now their relationship is even richer than before. Incidentally, they told me the movie was terrible and they laughed all the way through it, having a great time.

That's a living example of people who chose a positive, loving expression in the midst of negative temptation. They chose to go for the loving rather than the emotional upset.

You don't have to lay your annoyance on your mate. Instead, how about saying, "I've married you, and you can continue on just like you are if that's what you want because there's no demand from me to change. If I get annoyed when you do something, we'll both know it, and I'll make it my responsibility to love you through my annoyance."

In time, your annoyance might change to amusement and acceptance of your loved one's all-too-human conditioning. (Changing the attitude is a great key to having constructive, long lasting, loving relationships.) When you show that kind of unconditional loving, such a secure support may encourage your lover to change that habit just because of loving understanding. Not pressure. And even if they don't change, you are still experiencing love because you have chosen love.

PAIN, THE AWAKENER

When we give up our rights as individuals to other people, we are potentially opening the door to pain. In the traditional marriage vows of many years ago, the woman promised to "love, honor, and obey" her husband. The word "obey" connotes one consciousness being subservient to another, and any form of slavery can create resentment and pain.

Similarly, the marriage vows of "for better or for worse, for richer or for poorer" intimate responsibilities that you may be incapable of handling. Certainly, the "poorer … worse" parts are not your preference. A more aware preference might be that each one should not be a parasite or a leech upon the other, but be two people working together in mutual respect, cooperation, and lots of loving, with a liberal dash of humor to get through the difficult times.

Within a marriage, whenever your loved one takes any action, you are tied in some way to that action. For example, if the wife gets in debt, the husband has to pay the bill. If the husband bangs up his wife's car, her insurance company has to support the claim.

Instead of the romantic version of a marriage being two people head over heels in love with each other, staring blissfully into each other's eyes, I suggest a greater reality: two people looking in the same direction—not at each other—sharing a life path that can enrich and support both.

Another metaphor might be the husband as a pine tree and the wife as an oak tree. Neither can grow in the shadow of the other. They both have to stand far enough apart so the roots of one don't strangle the roots of the other. As they get taller, intermingling and sharing of beauty may take place, but at the bottom, where the stability lies, each must establish their own roots and foundation. You'd be further ahead to avoid the romantic fantasy and go for the reality. If you don't, you may create pain with the other and, certainly, for yourself.

People think that the easiest thing to do, in the short run, is to try to escape from pain, using whatever means possible: drugs; meaningless sex; excess food, alcohol or cigarettes; excessive time spent with television, books, or films—anything to get away from the pain, right? Because after all, why hang around in the pain that someone else is causing, right?

In the long run, however, trying to escape from pain is like trying to run away from yourself; it can't be done. You can go wherever you want, but the pain goes with you because pain is the response mechanism within you.

You may think, "But it's because of them. That's why I run away. I want to get away from them!" Of course, there may be times when it is a wise choice not to be with people who are expressing negativity. There may also be times when other choices may be even more beneficial to your growth. You might adopt another attitude and consider the possibility that someone else isn't the cause of your pain. Although it may seem as if your spouse is causing the pain by doing a certain thing, there is always another way of looking at the situation: just as the source of love is within you, so is the source of pain. When you experience pain, it is coming from a pain-full source within you.

You still might say, "I don't get it." My reply would be, "Yes, you do; you get your pain, but it isn't always your spouse's fault." Many people I know have been married and divorced numerous times and have had similar difficulties with each new marriage because it's the same old pattern. Their own negativity carried into each new relationship, and they perpetuated the pain by blaming the other.

Pain is just a method of recognition. Some people are willing to look, but few have the courage to see. If you are brave enough to see, you might recognize that the pain you are experiencing has more to do with you than with him or her. By placing the blame on him or her, you can be attempting to avoid the relationship within yourself.

I knew someone who used to go through anxiety attacks before a sporting event involving a favorite team. That person experienced extreme pain or pleasure, depending upon the outcome of the game. I experienced none of those things in relation to the same event. Was it the team that caused my friend's pain or pleasure?

If it was, then I should have had the same experience. It appeared to be a matter of each individual's attitude. It is clear that my friend's personal relationship with the event included emotional importance placed on the outcome of the game. My relationship with the same game was quite different. I didn't care who won or lost, yet I could enjoy watching the game.

Years later, I ran into this same friend and asked, "When that team loses, does it still drive you up the wall?" My friend responded, "No. Not anymore. I've outgrown that."

"Outgrown that" is very accurate. In other words, he needed to grow in order to recognize that his emotional reaction was his to own; in owning it, he could also discard it.

The same thing applies to your intimate relationship. When your spouse does that thing that can drive you up the wall, you can choose to outgrow it, not your spouse's action, but your reaction. You can do this if you are willing to own your reaction.

Owning it is another step toward awakening. Many people have allowed themselves to live a life in sleep. They seem to be walking through a nightmare of conditioned influences from their mother, father, society, gender expectations, financial background, sexual anticipations, fears, and everything but their original selves. We may as well face it: the history of planet Earth has not been seen as conducive to supporting original, loving, joyful abundance. Yet it is available for everyone who has the courage to go for it. How? Certainly not by blaming or by making them wrong or identifying them as the source of your pain. In order to awaken and activate the original you, you can start by accepting that the primary relationship in your life is with yourself. You can also realize that each of your emotional responses is yours to own and that you determine your attitude. What power you have! What a magnificent being you are! Are you willing and courageous enough to claim it?

JEALOUSY IN MARRIAGE

Jealousy works similarly to many other self-defense mechanisms, integrating many parts and precipitating an emotional reaction. If you try to handle just one part of the mechanism, it is usually ineffective. For instance, if you are jealous because you think your mate is flirting with someone else and if you divorce, in your next marriage, you may very well have to face a similar concern because of your intricate mechanisms.

It would serve you to first fix your "inner gears" that have become so well-oiled toward jealousy. Then, if someone does behave in a manner that doesn't work for you, you can deal with it as information, rather than through automatic emotional reactions to the mechanisms of the mind.

Jealousy is a process of vision, self-image, and imagination stemming from a weak self-concept. From that place of "I'm not really good enough" and "once my act is perceived, my mate will see my true lack of worthiness," you can create an image that supports that position of lack.

Jealousy is found primarily in the love relationships of someone who is experiencing a lack-of-love relationship with him or herself. Until a person does whatever it takes to recognize their true worth and value, every relationship can be hurt by jealousy. If people don't keep focused on the loving, they may fall into jealous accusations, often without proof, but with righteous emotion.

The dynamics of jealousy reveal not only a person's lack of trust for someone else but also a lack of trust for him or herself. The fear that they will lose their lover's love or that their lover will love someone else more is a driving force. Jealousy is a highly destructive force involving paranoia as a support system. I have seen extraordinary behavior from people trying to justify the jealousy that was actually covering their own unreliable behavior or their own insecurity, which has nothing to do with the other person. For example, I know of one husband who came home late from work, and when he went to flush the toilet, he noticed two cigarettes. He actually reached into the bowl to pull out the urine-soaked cigarettes in order to determine if the brand was his wife's.

I know of a wife who, when working late in the office, received a call from her husband asking what time she was coming home. She thought, "He never calls and asks that. He must have another woman in our house. Our bedroom. Our bed!"

She ran out before she finished the report she'd promised to have for her boss in the morning. She drove through the city like she was competing in the Indianapolis 500, barely missing a major accident. Two blocks before she got home, she turned off the car lights, and one block away, she put the gears in neutral so her husband wouldn't hear her arrive.

At the front door, she took off her shoes, tiptoed into the house and went directly into the bedroom, ready to catch them. No one was there. She heard a cork pop in the kitchen. "Ahh," she thought, "they're having a drink in the kitchen. Probably from that favorite wine we've been saving for a special occasion!"

She stormed into the kitchen, almost causing her husband to have a heart attack in surprise—only to find him there, fixing dinner for her. He had called her so he would have the surprise dinner all ready by the time she came home.

The wife was still stuck in jealousy as she said, "How did you get her out of here so fast? I can smell her perfume. How come you're cooking? Feeling guilty?" These acts are like paranoia. The best way to handle feelings of jealousy may be to share them with your mate, in honest vulnerability, not an accusation. You take responsibility for your feelings.

I know of one man who did that with his wife, and she just smiled and hugged him for caring so much. She sat near him, assuring him how much she loved him, and said, "Ask me any questions, darling, if you are still concerned about why I was late." In that simple way of giving him permission to ask, she diffused the concern. He asked, she answered, he felt better and apologized, and she just loved him for caring so much and being honest.

A woman can see a good-looking man and enjoy his appearance, and a man may appreciate something about another woman. They can enjoy and appreciate, but not participate, and if that is shared, even gender concerns can be transcended. For example, a couple can appreciate the beauty of another woman or another man, in person, on television, in the movies, or in a magazine. You can even play with each other about it with humor. If you're not going to have humor in your marriage, I suggest you reexamine your relationship because very few things on this planet can last without humor. Humor is often the only release from tension that cannot be resolved intellectually.

You can't cure jealousy by logical reasoning because it's not a logical, reasoning process. You and your partner have to demonstrate trust and unconditional loving by behavior. If you're unwilling to do that, you can be run by jealousy. If you two are physically separated, you don't have to imagine that your partner is involved with someone else. Instead, how about imagining that he or she is involved in some beautiful, loving, supportive action. Physical separation does not have to mean separation in loving each other.

Instead of giving in to the devious mechanisms of jealousy, as soon as it starts you can activate your awareness and choices. Don't let jealousy become just another habitual response.

Do what it takes to improve your own self-image. Do those things that give you an experience of your worth. These could include such things as ballet lessons, aerobics classes, the study of a foreign language, photography, greater expressions in service to the community—whatever works for you. Jealousy cannot survive in an atmosphere of worthiness, appreciation, and love. Instead of trying to solve the effect of jealousy, you can eliminate the cause by strengthening yourself.

BUILDING TRUST IN A RELATIONSHIP

Could you have a relationship with someone that you did not trust? Could you live with someone for what could be decades if you did not trust them? Trust is one of the main foundations of a long and healthy relationship. To build trust in a relationship can be fairly easy, especially at the start, the problem is, is that it is easy to lose that trust and if you do it will take a long time, and a lot of hard work to win it back again. If you really want to maintain and build trust in a relationship then you need to be totally open and honest with each other, for the rest of your time together, not everyone can do that and sadly not everyone wants to do that.

If you say that you will do something, then do it. It may sound pretty basic but it is fundamental to building trust, essentially what you are saying is that I give you my word that I will do this. It might be for something as simple as taking as taking the trash out, but if you do not do it after giving your word that you will then it knocks a bit of trust away. Once in a while people do forget, we are only human, in that case, regain the ground that you lost by taking responsibility for your actions and apologizing. If you are in a situation where you will be unable to do something because of having to work, being stuck in traffic and what have you, then let your partner know and do not close your eyes and hope that your partner has forgotten. For those who are tempted to come up with creative explanations please remember that your body language will probably give you away, your partner will notice this and their trust in you will diminish. If you keep, "forgetting" to do things then you are showing that you are not serious about the relationship, that you do not treat your partner with respect and that your word is worthless.

Everyone gets into a routine. For example, Joe works Monday to Friday, he leaves the house at 8 in the morning and is back by 6. On the weekends he spends some time with his wife and kids and meets up with friends on a Saturday night for a few drinks. Joe has a wife called Josephine, she knows his routine and what to expect. Then all of a sudden he has to start working late and working weekends, he takes more care of his image, he starts getting back home in the early hours of the morning. Josephine, strangely enough, is suspicious at this break from what is normal. Suspicion if left unchecked is a terrible thing that can poison an individuals mind and wreck a relationship. Any deviation from what is predictable can if repeated often enough destroy trust in you. If your routine is set to change then do the courteous thing and let your partner know. People continually change and if there is something where you are likely to have a significant change from the norm then tell your partner.

You need to give your partner a reason to trust you to share your lives with them. Now in a loving, healthy, fulfilling relationship, communication plays a major part in forging a connection between you and keeping it strong. When you share your day, your hopes, your dreams and your emotions you are giving your partner the key to who you are, this shows that you trust them and that more than anything will really build trust between you.

When you have problems then work at them together to find a compromise or solution that you are both happy with. Do not try and point score of each other, you are equal partners with equal responsibilities for making your relationship work. Show that you care about what happens to you both and take whatever actions you need to help your relationship.

To build trust in a relationship you need to accept your partner for who they are, they are who you fell for so do not try to change them into something that they are not. Realize and accept that your partner as a separate individual will have their own opinions and even if you do not agree with them, still treat them with respect. Do not keep secrets from each other, nothing will destroy a relationship as quickly as one or both of you having secrets. Living a lie is not a healthy way to live and your body language will give you away. Be open and honest with your partner and as your relationship grows then so will your trust for each other.

Things That Builds Trust In Couples Relationship

1. Honesty

One of the things another person will look for when deciding if you are trustworthy is personal honesty. They will weigh what you say against what you do and they will also look to see if you are being honest with yourself. If you want to gain someone else's trust, it is a good time to look at the areas of your life you have been avoiding. It is a good time to seek out and confront denial. Many times people will lament, "Why don't you trust me? I'm being honest." What they mean is they are telling the truth to another person at this moment. True honesty deals with how much our inner and outer lives match. Honesty is a quality you develop first with yourself and then with the greater world. If someone is telling you they still can't trust you, both of you need to focus on developing honesty and trust with yourselves before you can share it as a couple.

2.   Vulnerability

Confronting denial can be really scary stuff, especially when the other person in the relationship is not offering much of themselves. It can make you feel really vulnerable. Wanting to hide when you feel that vulnerable is understandable. If you want to grow trust with your partner, though, it is time to share those feelings even when they're scary. Especially because they're scary. Being able to say things like "I'm afraid", "I want...", and "I feel..." without expecting the other person to reciprocate transmits genuine trustworthiness.

3.   Communication

You might do all this inner work and become a very trustworthy person, but if there is no communication with your partner, there will still be no reason for them to trust you. It is worthwhile to learn how to communicate well. Communication is not simply stating what you want and how you feel, no matter what. It involves listening to the other person, thinking about the way you say things, and having a back-and-forth dialogue with your partner where you each pause, listen and give feedback before moving on.

4.   Mutuality

This step speaks of give and take. You need to give to the other person what you would like in return. It also speaks of having mutual respect. Respect yourself and your partner and expect respect in return. Set boundaries and stick to them. That means doing what you say you will, but it also means not allowing someone to treat you with disrespect. You cannot control someone else's actions, but you can say: this is not okay, and I am going to my room until we can be civil.

5.   Affection

Part of building trust is expressing how we feel for each other. Expressing love and genuine affection for someone else lets them know they can trust the words you are saying because you are also expressing genuine affection. Play together, enjoy each other. Building trust is not all serious business. In fact, if you leave lightness out of it, there won't be much reason to grow or save the relationship at all. Play to your strengths. Work with what works, as well as what doesn't. And take your time. Trust will grow when it is ready, and you will both be much stronger for it.

TRICKS THAT WORK

How do you keep the loving going on a practical one-to-one relating level when things get sticky? (And there will probably be times when they do get sticky, if not downright rough.) In other words, how do you translate the concept of unconditional loving into living actions? When things are hellish, how do you invoke heaven?

Practice. Use any and everything to get yourself into that active, loving state. Besides such things as contemplation, meditation, spiritual exercises, workshops, seminars, uplifting literature, and so on, you can invent your own methods.

Some people use a symbol on a necklace that indicates loving. Others have a ring. Some have something in their pocket that was a precious gift of love, or they may even wear a rubber band on their wrists that they snap as a stinging reminder to avoid negativity. Of course, these are only physical objects, which have no inherent power. They, however, symbols of your intention; they are your methods, your reminder.

I have seen people use those physical objects when the pressure is on. When you are inclined to go for one of those you-said-I-said-you-did-I-did routines, making the other person wrong and exploding in righteous indignation, take a second and just physically touch that object. In that physical touch, think of the loving it represents. Run your anger and your emotional reaction through that object, and see if it dissolves. You can use that inanimate object to reawaken your loving power. Does it work? It can if you work it.

You've heard the expression "count to ten before you talk," meaning do what it takes while you're in an emotional state to center yourself. That actually works for some people. Others have to count to one hundred before they get centered. Some people have a word or a phrase that they repeat silently when they get into one of those "off-center" states. If you choose such a keyword or phrase, it's best to choose something when you are flowing with love. Then that word or expression will naturally have the loving energy. When you call on it during an upset period and repeat it as long as is necessary to receive of the loving energy, your emotional upset can be transformed into neutral observation, acceptance, and even warm, human love. A trick? Perhaps, but anything that evokes loving has value.

One person I know uses a particular piece of music (Pablo Casals playing Bach on the cello), which immediately settles him down, soothes him, and helps him reconnect to his beautiful loving heart.

Find those tricks that work for you, and then work them. Living on this planet is sometimes tricky. Why not be a great magician? Be an alchemist, and transform negativity into loving. It's possible. You can even involve your mate in this technique, and you both may play the love-trick game.

I know two lovers who received a pair of beautiful Dresden figurines as a wedding gift. They kept these dolls on a table in the bedroom. If one person was upset or angry with the other, they would go into the bedroom and turn one doll so its back was to the other.

When the other went to the bedroom and saw this, they recognized there was a problem. Of course, a traditionally conditioned person might turn the other doll around so there would be two dolls with their backs to each other, imitating two human beings.

Fortunately, this couple chooses to solve problems rather than be run by emotional conditioning. And their problems did become very difficult at times, almost getting to the point of their not wanting to sleep in the same bed.

It never got that far, however, because they had a prior agreement by which each abided. That commitment was that if one of those Dresden dolls faced away from the other, they would not go to sleep until each one would be able to turn the dolls face to face. Of course, this meant that the two human beings would face each other and talk it out. Sometimes it might take most of the night and they wouldn't get to sleep until 4:00 a.m. But even though they had to get up at 7:00 a.m. in order to get to work on time, when they did awaken with the dolls facing each other, they also awakened with incredible energy. Each recognized that the thing going on in this world that was worth the most was the exchange of loving energy.

This isn't a theoretical exchange of energy. I am talking about specifics. Sometimes a working person will come home with dirt on their shoes, leaving tracks on the floor. Their spouse may clean the floor afterward, understanding that dirt is okay and can be cleaned up. Sometimes the person will take off their shoes first.

There are more difficult conflicts, of course—those times when two approaches to an issue are seemingly incompatible and there doesn't seem to be a viable compromise or middle ground. Many people have divorced because of the inability to find a solution, while others have remained in a marriage of acrimony.

There is a third choice. You can take those things that are not working and actually move them outside the relationship. In a way, you put them in a museum. You can give each issue a name. In your imagination or in reality, if that's possible, you can take a photograph of it, a sculpture, or a symbolic item and put it in a glass case or in a cardboard box in the garage. You can write the name in a book that has a lock and key and put the book away.

The technique is for both of you to agree not to disagree; you both commit to making this a non-issue. You two make it not available for conflict by literally putting it away in storage, someplace that you both declare as off limits. As a result of this agreement, you never involve yourself in that "thing" in your relationship.

If you both go for this arrangement, it can have a remarkable bonding effect. As a result of your mutual agreement to "put it on the shelf" and to make it unavailable for conflicting approaches, you have made a commitment to solidify your living relationship with each other.

Will that issue ever be dealt with? Sometimes the issue will dissolve because of lack of energy. When something isn't fed, it often fades away. Then again, there are those "things" that can be kept "on the shelf" until there is a safe time and a safe place to deal with them. Don't be premature in taking them off the shelf. Be sure you both make an agreement —even if it's to keep it there for ten years—and stick to it.

The important thing about this technique is to keep the issue outside the relationship. That may seem to be a difficult concept to grasp, but if relationships were easy, you might not be reading this book.

Just for clarity, consider that there are many significant issues and events that are outside your relationship. For instance, there are satellites floating in outer space; there is a man fishing on a lake in the Soviet Union; there is a koala bear in a tree in Australia; there is night in another part of the world when you are having daytime. All of these things are outside your relationship, and there is nothing you can or should do about any of them. Put that seemingly unresolvable conflict with your mate at a similar distance.

Of course, your mind may tell you that it is not so, that the issue, the "thing," is right here and gnawing away at you. If you want a successful relationship, you might learn how to discipline the mind so that it holds a focus on what you want, rather than react to mental constructs that may not have much to do with your heart.

The likelihood is that if you have successfully kept your agreement to keep the "thing" locked away, and then you have dusted it off for review at the given time you both agreed on—ten months, ten years, whatever it is—the energy on it will no longer have a negative charge. In fact, it may actually have turned into a museum piece, a relic to view with interest as a representative of another time long since gone.

What "thing" in your relationship consistently causes separation regardless of mutual attempts at a solution? Only you can determine that. It may vary from expectations of physical proportions ("she's too fat"), attitudes toward relaxation time ("he only wants to go to the movies" or "she always wants to eat at the same restaurant"), or money, or anything else that you create as a conflict between the two of you.

Demands and expectations can lead to separation. If you both agree to put your demands in the museum, you are left with only acceptance and togetherness, which is the whole point of marriage anyhow.

Your mind may be arguing, "Doesn't putting it into a museum mean stuffing it? Doesn't the issue go into the unconscious whether you're dealing with it up front or not?" It doesn't matter where it goes. By putting your righteous positions on the shelf, you are giving your heart the time to dissolve or resolve the conflict.

Some problems don't have to be solved by actions or words. Time will solve some problems in and of itself. This museum technique is calling on time and loving, which some people call Spirit, to resolve the differences you two may have created long before your conscious memories. It can happen if you are strong and loving enough to get out of the way and let Spirit work in Its own perfect timing.

HOW COUPLES CAN ENSURE A MEANINGFUL AND HAPPY LIFE TOGETHER

Have you ever wondered, how married couples, who truly love each other, stay together and seem to love each other even more? or How they do it and what's their secret? I guess if it could all be answered in just a couple of sentences, everybody would be doing it, this article would end here, and we'd be done and dusted, package delivered, I'm out - peace.

Unfortunately for me, we're only just starting.

Your marriage began the second you said "I DO", to the person, you loved to bits and you knew would always be there for you for the rest of your life. But how do couples keep the love alive in a marriage and the passion burning HOT? Firstly it is highly important that before you both tie the knot in marriage, that you both, personally know what you have in common and what you don't, what weaknesses you possess and what strengths you have. Before the marriage has actually started, it makes good sense to know how to recognize problems that may arise and how to handle them. The sacred marriage vows, couples promise to each other should be remembered and honored for all time.

Although couples enter into a marriage looking forward to a wonderful and prosperous future, they will undertake problems, conflicts, and struggles. Struggles that will test the couple's relationship, even to the point of breaking. Marriages can be ripped apart from the struggles it will experience or as the old saying goes, anything that doesn't kill (the relationship) will only make it stronger, both the relationship and the married couple. Couples will need to rely on each other to deal with all problems and disagreements encountered along the way.

Now-days though, when married couples are confronted with conflicts, they tend to bail out of the marriage immediately, rather than work things out. To sidestep this reality, and help rescue and protect your marriage before its too late, here are some pointers and advice that you might need to know.

During any conflict, dilemma, struggle or argument - consultation and communication are paramount. Listen to what your spouse is saying to you. Listen, listen, listen and no matter what else you do, don't cut them off while they are speaking, don't try to solve the problem, before you have heard all of the facts and don't be negative and cause any more arguments, as this will hinder your progress. Listen to your partner with an open and understanding mind and a loving heart. Sometimes your partner may need your understanding that, you don't have to solve all their problems all of the time, and that they may just need you to hear them out, be supportive or tell them that you are sorry for whatever issue it is they are going through or that you are sorry, they are struggling to find the words, they need to express and explain their situation or that you are sorry, they are having great difficulty trying to draw on the courage, they need to deal with, whatever it is they are experiencing at this difficult time. We all need to be loved and supported by our partners. We need our partners to be our sounding board, and vent to them any thoughts, frustrations or problems, we may have bottled up or get off our chest any issues or dislikes that are stressing us out. With this said, we also need our beloved partners to give them a big hug and tell us that everything will be alright.

Be strong and remain positive. When the marriage is fresh and new and the couples have a strong attraction to one another, they pay attention to the cute little things each other does but over time, without warning, the couple starts to notice little things that stand out, that they don't like or becomes a nuisance, annoying and an inconvenience to say the least. To avoid the drama of a huge marriage break up, couples need to remember when they first fell in love with each other, or the cute little things each other did when their marriage was new, whatever you do, don't complain.

Complaining to your partner or directly at them, all of the time is like being continually kicked in the guts, not a good look, not good at all. Too much nagging and complaining can cause them to switch off from listening - making them really angry, frustrated and hurt. The best approach you could take is the higher ground, by communicating your selected choices of complaints to your partner, delivered in a positive, constructive manner, so they don't feel intimidated, offended or embarrassed. At all times remain cool, calm and collected and don't forget to give merit, when merit is due to your partner for their mature attitude towards issues you've raised, the positive wise qualities they contribute to the relationship and the understanding only the person whom you love and adore would possess.

Spend a lot of quality time together and both of you will appreciate each others company and become closer in the process. Don't just limit yourselves to talk about your problems while your spending time on outings, or on dates - your together time to talk about those issues should happen all the time. It's important to talk about positive things as well, mixing the negative issues with the positive ones, is a good thing, nobody wants to hear the negatives all the time - too depressing. So communicate your fears and concerns to your partner, just remember to mix the positives with the negatives, throughout your discussions and conversations and you'll be fine. Whatever you do, don't get caught up on talking to your partner about the petty little problems, you encounter at work, you have with family or friends. That's a negative trap for married couples, you'd never want to get stuck in that predicament, it could take years to get out of and change.

Remember that sex was a huge part of when you first met and it made the relationship exciting, riveting and exhilarating. Don't forget to be intimate and affectionate. Make time to show your true affections for each other and remember that having a happy relationship, doesn't just revolve around having tons of sex.

We only live once, so live in the moments that take your breath away with the ones we love, treasure those memories forever.

Treasured memories, where you spend time together at home, snuggled together on the couch or sleeping in together on the weekends or holding hands while your walking down the street or in a mall or taking baths or showers together or a gentle kiss on the neck or massaging the tense muscles of your loved one or a light peck on the cheek. It's about connecting with one another, emotionally, touching each other in a non-sexual way. Through physical contact in a non-sexual way, you exhibit the true connection and love, you have for each other.

*If You have a few moments, I would appreciate a review on **Amazon**, if You found your new book useful in any way.*

© *Copyright 2021 by **SARAH SULLIVAN***